Landscapes :: Bodies

Sneha Subramanian Kanta

HAWAKAL

Published by Hawakal Publishers
185 Kali Temple Road, Nimta, Kolkata 700049

Email: info@hawakal.com
Website: www.hawakal.com

First edition: April, 2019

Copyright © Sneha Subramanian Kanta 2019
Cover art: Sufia Khatoon
Cover designed by Bitan Chakraborty

ISBN: 978-93-87883-53-6

Price: INR 200.00 | USD7.50

for

nani, my parents, & Harsh

"like a new word I learned and embraced,
like the everday jug,
like my mother's face,
like a ship that carried me along
through the deadliest storm."

Rainer Maria Rilke

Preface

In the summer of 2017 Rhythm Divine Poets initiated, perhaps, India's first ever poetry chapbook contest. This ambitious project was to recognize and publish new and upcoming poets. The winners were Huzaifa Pandit and Kripi Malviya and their respective books, *Green is the Colour of Memory* and *Ale(theia)* were published by Hawakal Publishers. In its second year (2018) the contest saw participation from numerous poets from all over the world making it one of the most anticipated contests to look forward to by potential participants.

Rhythm Divine Poets, co-founded by the three Kolkata-based poets Amit Shankar Saha, Sufia Khatoon and Anindita Bose, is happy that over a period of four years since its inception, it has successfully worked for the promotion of poetry through various activities like events, workshops, publications, and its flagship project of the poetry chapbook contest, all of which gives platforms to young and aspiring poets. The group has utilized the advantages of social networks like WhatsApp, Facebook and Blog (http://rhythmdivinepoets.blogspot.in) to create the so-called "poetry scene" in Kolkata, making its presence felt in India, and bringing it on par with the world.

Rhythm Divine Poets Poetry Chapbook Contest in its second edition has been privileged to have judges from Intercultural Poetry and Performance Library (IPPL – http://ipplkolkata.wordpress.com). The panel included eminent academicians and poets, Prof. Sanjukta Dasgupta, Dr. Sharmila

Ray, Dr. Jaydeep Sarangi, Ms. Joie Bose, Dr. Naina Dey, Ms. Ananya Chatterjee and Dr. Sutapa Chaudhuri. It was a keenly contested competition and any of the seven shortlisted poets (Anupam Sinha from Dresden, Germany, Sana Tamreen Mohammed from USA, Kinshuk Gupta from Haryana, Nikita Parik and Rita Bhattacharjee from West Bengal, Sawmitra Roy from Assam, and Sneha Subramanian Kanta from Mumbai, India) could have emerged as a winner.

One of the judges, Naina Dey, said about her experience of judging the manuscripts: "Shortlisting submissions inevitably proved to be a challenging exercise. However, poetry requires skillful wordplay, a command over language to express both the concrete and the abstract so the mind can glide smoothly over each line while taking in the nuances of meaning like an eagle's wings skimming the water as its beak deftly lifts the flailing fish. Thus we have a poem in which spontaneity is coupled with precision, emotion coupled with word, image coupled with message – a poem that speaks to the readers for the readers – a winning poem." For Sanjukta Dasgupta: "It has indeed been a matter of immense pleasure and rich learning experience to have been given the opportunity to evaluate the poems entered for the chapbook contest. The sameness and difference in the themes and variations, substance and style, in the enthusiastic submissions from all over the world, carry the singular message that poetry effectively builds bridges of cultural understanding." Rhythm Divine Poets group thanks all the judges from IPPL, especially Prof. Sanjukta Dasgupta, Dr. Naina Dey and Ms. Joie Bose for devoting their time to judge the contest.

The group also thanks the venue partner, for the longlisting and shortlisting events, Alliance Française du Bengale, and especially its Director, Mr. Fabrice Plançon. The group owes its debt of gratitude to Hawakal Publishers who has published the winning chapbook. And thanks are also due to all those who came in support of the endeavour. Rhythm Divine Poets wishes the winner, Sneha Subramanian Kanta, the very best in her poetic journey in life.

RDP
Kolkata
March, 2019

Contents

Tethered by Borders

The space aboriginals find home in is soon lost
thereafter; it never belonged to them. Their woe,
the dream of governments, the nightmare of politicians.

Press conferences quibble in placards of justice handed –
smudged in red ink over a white cardboard surface,
as though a widowed woman in India dare wore *sindoor*.

There are things one is denied by virtue of birth – those
that stick to them entire life, as an uncalled birthmark.
I have seen militants draw a line of control, patrolling

during the wee hours of night: the owl hoots, insects
sleepily crawl over marshes of white chalk scribbling:
like teaching in silent sermons the value of borderless

spaces. Still, we're taught to measure prosperity in other
quantum: the import and export in shared extra margins –
while an old woman lying in the corner cries in the cold.

Lineage

I was Ahilya
standing by the Jhelum
out-stretched were landscapes
of *shikaras* and
a forlorn post office.

Nobody has come here
since many yesterdays
the two rupee note is
archaic, and safely ignored.

Baba tells me this is *kalyug* –
saints won't open their eyes,
nor will the world resurrect;
while I play with a white dove.

Bambai

The city is a cusp
        suspended between
a nocturnal hum
of balmy orange streetlights and
the *barah baje ki* local

sleep does not know
the idea of a lodging.

Outside, the night air is filled
with *beedi* fumes
a soot of pollution and
        smells of unfulfilled
dreams that linger below the irises,
        darkened skin patches
        of a tired homemaker.

It breathes
it moves
it shifts,
constantly, like the sea.
        We talk of God as though
a man, then worship
        women deities.

It is a land of paradoxes
                yet life exists
                in the anticipatory *shanties*
the *jhopad-patti* has got enough coverage

                in first world movies.

The concrete roads
                are full of anxiety
too many have walked over its surface.
                It stings of nylon threads
used in garlands to cover dead bodies.

Our skins have become purple like gloaming
                we have internalized
                little girls portraying acrobatics
                on a thin thread,
                using a thicker thread to dry clothes,
                unfunny television comedies.

Autorickshaw-wallahs still play 90's songs,
                barbers and taxi drivers can tell you more
                about politics than your local corporator.

There are symbols spread
all over the place: school,
                mandir, church, *gurudwara*,
etcetera. The roads have become narrower

                rivers have been chopped down to cover costs
                of profitable municipalities.

                The city is an interlude
between breathing and the conscious,
                the *junta* and *paani*,
                at the end we all seem like flies statically
                hovering over a brown cup of *chaai*.

At night a bird perched on my window

and chirped. Restless, indignant fellow roaming rims of night
tides surge and cascade, plummet. Nobody will say four a.m. is the
time to expect birds in winter, on the longest night of the year.

It's not as though *tsuris* arrived just now amid white noise
my bones crack with the weight of toil as the feral creature
basks in a swathe where I listen to the hymns of birdsong

far across the land I sense poppies unbutton before dawn dew.
The spirit flows away into a reserve in evanescence as night
slowly softens into day, emptying earth of stray noises,

the pastoral highlights: cattle, tractor engines, farmers tilling lands
as a crimson shaped orb overwrites color on fronds
small fishes in the river have been stealing silver from the moon.

A Reminiscence: In Homage of

My grandmother, hair carefully parted, the analogy of
symbolism of Karachi tracing routes into a camp at

Ulhasnagar. Her eyes, the dreams of her brothers and
sister, carefully outlined in the papyrus of irises, thickly

inscribed in deft hands, tying my hair in two neat plaits.
As a small girl with borders inflicted on palm lines,

passed sea-creatures as they slithered beneath waves;
aboriginal names of areas in Karachi safely stationed

within the pleats of her *pallu* as time or whatever else it is,
ran its course, an alchemical winding of fibers between

a ballpoint and an ink pen.

She died inside when my grandfather died. The rhythm of
his death struck deep inside her belly: ravenous sky, in the

dark of an anvil where she often told me Shiv would come
to her rescue. The rabbits of hours dispersed in blank *tandav*

and linger among the dots and pores of frozen skin.

old Goa
for H

you showed me the bright sun – it shone as a spot of gold
dust – the ramifications
of history did not damage planets. we clung on to each other
– cocooned in a thin
layer of fabric – your hands with leftover oil – from coastal
food, my feet soles
with sand granules. you took me to the corner of Benaulium
beach – broken shells
were washed ashore – our corner of shells – see, how the sea
saves nothing for itself.

you were a soliloquy in yourself – away from the maddening
crowd – I was pulled
by your gravitation – seagulls took flight into the vast, one
layered blue sky.

the light tinge of moon – visible on an afternoon – captured
by your lens – while
a man played the violin. your eyes – brushstrokes of
observation – we sat down on
broken stairs, listening to muffled voices – the silences in
open, unoccupied spaces

were inviting. a bicycle cast a shadow of its own – then
basked in the sun. outside
my own being – there was you – an extension of my
breathing self. I realized you

were the openness, the vast sky, sounds of birds and the
texture of sand. you were
the force of life – gushing through my bloodstream – I
realized – the reason to live.

Passion

on straddling stratospheres of a shore lone
weary waters wild unuttered coruscating coastlines
schlep waves. aloft draped waves dissolving sand
drench scarves of wind. foamy froth ventriloquist,
the shaded moon waltzes sophist like to tides.
blazing inflame these synecdoches pellucid, variable
almanac vicissitudes. the bedding of heady air thick
with water minerals build and glisten. intensifying
and receding abundant bubbling of provinces leap.
thrilling coats of relentless, working sounds.

through luminosity of vacuum reflecting radiant are
dangling weather intricacies, airborne with fibres
of untiring momentum over warm days and overnight.
the grains of constancy inherit myriad multitudes in
amalgamating fluid. winding and unwinding cadences
of unwavering discrepancies on fine line residual patches.
mistier substances wreathe rendering shrill stroking the
sibilant plumage drowned unequivocally. gathering
surges heightening cascade back and forth. burnished
glowing tinges forming at all directions on-ward.

Yarns of Shapes

I have never been good at math since late school
but know a fair bit of geometry. Sometimes, I trace
shapes & stick collages of dead flowers into them
& look at shadows they form over lined paper.
One afternoon, a sparrow stood into the white space

between a hexagonal contour over the window grid
& I thought of residuals left by afternoons as some
kind of inheritance for women who waited by panes
& felt like the earth rotated three hundred & sixty-six
times in a day but did not spare them a timeless hour.

Now looking through the low-grades & night sweats
I want to say to my tutor that not all scars have a name
for the shape they are formed in: the calculus of
undulant sorrow. I did not know formulae but the
rosary would become circle & square at the same time.

Zelda

"She refused to be bored chiefly because she wasn't boring."
Zelda Fitzgerald

Zelda, unbeknownst sister of Ozymandias
accompany me to where the sun rises
east of Baghdad, west of Byzantium

let us make our spot for pilgrimage there.
Rub fertile mud on our skin whilst
the approving sun shines –

I, your brown sister, will bring you tales
from the other side of the Mississippi
you tell me about the Americas

you have seen in one country.
To speak of roots and corkscrews,
bottles and potions, we will read

Rumi to find out how much the heart
can hold. Beyond the yellowing
sand dunes, let us recall the last bird

who sang in the middle of a desert.
What shall we plant here, in the middle
of a heatstroke land – cacti, seeds of

wild blueflowers, or do we bury
carols for Christmas?

The Unburied

"The difference between a path and a road is not only the
obvious one."

–Wendell Berry

Now, the unburied mumble a song.
Nobody knows why it is dear to them.

Summer dusk, warmer than other months
is not ideal for ferns to grow greener.
Aware, they prepare for another fate.

The unburied sing –
their decibel cuts through a winter night
left with excesses of fissure fragments.

Now, the unburied lay on a footpath
resemble Dadaist art.

This physical place of empty roads
material capillaries of dark roads –
under a flyover you see them slumber

their eyes beget the shape of early dreams
burnt with autumn leaves.

The municipal is commissioned
to wipe leaves that fall on the road
as though to clear space for an unknown fate.

Now, the unburied remove food
from a polythene
in the wee hours of night,

light a fire and watch their reflection
in the incandescent flame
along a coast that shimmers with

yellow streetlamps and children
imagine the sea as free as a butterfly.

How does the fluttering of a closed heart
sound, like birds flap their wings
while allowing a moment for flight.

Now, the unburied amid ashen hue winds
rise from underbellies of roads.

How my father prays

See, how moths eat dark
devour dusk contours
               like raised fragments from a cashmere shawl.
Call me Ishmael, I tell my father
               speak to me in a mouth full of Persian dialects
mumble

               but my father is a silent man of great faith
in God. He tells me the ship is at a certain distance from land
because God wills it so.
Upon the knee of a ghazal
               in pastiche stitched emulsifications of synapse ships
the sea is vacant like land
               there is no grimoire, nor the steady onslaught
of rain.

My father supervises the symmetry
               of a small-lodging night room in the ship,
               I ask him of the openness of space and the shape
of stars. He cusps his hand in prayer and points etherward.
Dawn disseminates in soft pores
               over ancillaries of his phalange as the warm sun
rises eastward.

The ceiling of the ship lathers with froth formed dayclouds
my father withdraws to a quiet spot
        with psalms from a Dravidian text
invokes God from the mosaic of skies,
        and then breaks bread.

Notes de jonction

One day your teeth feel softer against the push of your jaws. It seems like you have woken up in someone else's body: the quiet pulsating nerve presses upon the skin like the edges of a rivulet. I am told that identity exists, but I learn it is as futile as it forms. The whole form of life is distorted, like the sounds from the engine of a static train on the sidetrack of a huge field. The juice from roses which leans upon the spine of a hardback meanders in search of elsewhere. The skeleton conjoins a body and is remade again. There are no codes for where you belong, only post office numbers or pin codes. I dwell between two narrow lanes where peace resides: nobody looks at you to draw blood from your thighs that are tall and thick like the diameter of a waterfall. We are used to algorithms, not voices of the body. You can blame the city but municipal councils do not come with warning signs. There is an entire continent dwelling upon one grain of froth like the padding inside deep sea beds. I write a letter with semantic coherence and place it upon a wave over the deep blue sea. There is no language inscribed upon its body: it was drenched and moved along lines swarming entire continents.

Nitya

for Kanta, my mother

I walked by the sea-shore, with reverberating sounds
from Eliot's Wasteland and its usage of Sanskrit words

and remembered my mother and I going to learn the
language.

It was evening even then — inscribed in an elegiac meter;
the soul was eternal, time; ever-changing and temporal.

The teacher, a long white-bearded fellow, an off-spring of
the *samsara*, turned away by its own cocoon often paid emphasis

on syllables that must be stressed upon — like some natural
emergency beckoned attention. My mother, a connoisseur of

languages and linguistics, carefully took notes. How we walked
the lane to our abode in the government quarters, her *hrit pundarika*

beating fast to the pace of incomplete chores — my *stotram* for her,
unknown to her, still incomplete.

Nani

I see her sometimes, arising from folds of dark, hair left loose like tresses of cypress trees, holding an earthen lamp. Eyes lined in straight, neat kohl lines with enough light to illuminate curvature contours of her face. The last time I saw her wear a red *saree* was when *nana* was alive, but in flashes like these, I only see a silhouette of her face. I have yearned to meet a goddess after my mother's death & have come to learn of grief as strength. Her face, pristine as morning sun reflects memory at night—the night she doesn't come to visit becomes *amavasya*. If night is an elegy with melancholic sounds, then dawn is the numb hour when psalms from her marooned breath find way into my eardrums. If all light is god & god rises with the sun, she turns day into night & rises with the moon. The smell of an ocean lingers on her body. I see her without the grief I last saw on her face, after losing a daughter & being caged. I want to ask if she traveled back to Karachi to look at her ancestral house abandoned during partition & if all light is the shape of god. She leaves by turning into the shape of a diamond, gliding like a bird through gleams of space in the blue cirrocumulus.

J. Alfred Prufrock's Letter to his Brown Cousin

The blue sea and white foam mix as Picasso's
color palette, but it has different veins. At noon,
I rolled my flannel trousers in three folds, then
wiped snow off the window rails stuck there
like white wax. There was a flood outside but I
preferred the company of plants that grow when
it rains outside. I brought bread, candles, envelopes.
The stamps and paper were in stock. Who thinks
of how things in the house were placed while they
read a letter? Perhaps there is a haphazard link.
I am full of unwanted details. The sink is clean like
shallow water in monsoon. I saw greenshanks scatter
by the bay while smells of cement sprinted from the sea.
Does a year add anything to increase written volumes?
I end with a philosophical anecdote and hope it shines
on the page for you to learn. We are descendants
from the same fate. I ask you to touch a tattered
cloud from the sky when it rains on the other side.

Matunga Central

(i)

afternoon

the coarse brown-grayness
of a *bhakri* on his plate —
mispronounced in the street

he was born in an era
where yellow newspapers
outlined a sun's beam.

(ii)

evening

today, hurried commuters
full of sweaty armpits
chase the six thirty local,

disturb his surprised peace.
the old man breathes this
anxious air, wipes his

spectacles to look —
at speckles of tired,
worn-out, undead faces.

(iii)

night

dust has settled everywhere
a few particles on his spectacles —
he still sees the mosaic

of squished fruits and vegetables
abandoned in the dark,
in silent acceptance of their fate.

(iv)

midnight

he rolls the makeshift carpet
pachaas rupaiya daily wage,
burdened by the reflection

of railway pillars, sounds
of a distant Coimbatore express,
walking towards the station

platform. municipal workers
gather to assimilate dust in
their lungs and the remainder

in bins.

(v)

dawn

an excruciating sunrise
delayed by a quarter
lurks around the city

uninhabited, with its quiet,
rustic leftovers. monuments
stoic with cold surfaces.

he prepares to sleep
on a tattered blanket —
the treasured steel trunk

is fast asleep beneath the
wooden bed, full of stamps,
black and white photographs

and daily wage. he offers
his wage to the feet of two
bronze idols of gods before

pulling the blanket over.

Sepia Night

emergencies   are   haphazard vacations
       (you aligned them with the lint of august)

post-truth of *Nietzsche*
like snake-skins clad,
           slithering past the lone forest
           filling with noise of rustlings.

     the   reflections   over your eyelash –
       shadowed over my body
in perpetual Calcutta heat, as the Hooghly streamed on.

Fenollosa manuscript

You train me in Japanese art forms
and diverge into the world of being:
not sea-swarmed by illegitimates,
as postmodern newspapers claim.

The politikal language is loosening
itself in distilled embers.

Unbecoming, as you placed your
hand within my palm, once –
within the amniotic fluid of a forest,
the reserve of bees and small fish.

We set tidal waves in the grove
against evening, and ourselves,

to unmoor.

The Violence in Our Bones
after Amrita Pritam

It is strange how violence
makes a home out of itself

in our bones, passed from
grandmother to granddaughter

as a legacy, hidden in our dupattas,
as silence while pickling mangoes.

Summer sky, cotton candy clouds
the koi circumnavigate the temple pond

in search for peace & glide over
to the surface of water.

Unfair land disallows them entry
often, death is the price for migration.

I know the word for violence in
four languages: Hindi, Urdu, Sindhi, Tamil

but it remains an inaccessible tongue.
On vacant nights while peeling off

coconut husks or sticking cow-dung
over side-walls in the village hut,

I hear the mountains
call to mingle with their habitat,

to be unrestrained & solitary.
a bloodless moon is blanched every amavasya.

Don't ask me to tip henna on my
cuticles, don't bring me to a strange

city after I garland you because
it doesn't mean I make a god out of you.

I have made an exile of my body
in the past, in the transcendence of nights.

My grandmother told me how she saw
thousands of people line by gigantic ships

to flee land. Nobody puts their young
on a voyage in the sea for fear of shipwreck

but the brave or the fearful. Her chest has grown
like a banyan tree since, she said, as I looked

at her willowy frame. Mogras and roses adorn
her hair—I inhale their aromas at dawn.

Ghazal for my grandmother

Then again, the pale moon comes out: blood soon replaced with
                                       hope
traced in the mapless cocoon of fractured geography, swallows
                                       hope.

Though the night is black — with moths, its fangs open in silver —
lines of peoples reflect its copper-toothed, velvety aura,
                                    wait for hope.

The land split in abandoned houses and shadows of the dead
the swollen blue sea with lines of canoes, leading to distant ships.
                                    Hope.

Child undone with shadowgreen scarf, windswept hair, I see you
graze your fingers as the boat unmoors, wear an organ of hope.

The sea is tea-stained at a distance, gurgles with the throat of an owl
amid a cobra tinted night with marigolds
                                 in your hair for good omen.
                                 Hope.

Expressionism

how you eat the fallen figs
your body full of soil scents –
arm clutched to my side,
bare bodies of autumn's pride.

your fingers, opening a map –
nail pointing eastward
moving subtly, then all at once
over the body of the large Pacific.

how your mouth, partly open
devours my mouth, in exploration –
then, like ancient forest-dwellers
sing ourselves to sleep, meditating.

how chants, escape your tongue,
lick my senses into molten clay –
how, in a world of immigrants,
we find – a land unknown, to stay.

lines

Mumbai. formerly Bombay,
2017 A.D.
the city of a breathing sea
divided invisibly
mutilated river
drying dead
third world fellow countrymen
smoking *beedis*
walking subways
of Chhatrapati Shivaji Terminus
constant dystopia
first world slavery
new bridges
link roads
gaps of lines
between the sea
poverty cries
in close cloisters
slum dwellings
five year old selling *chaai*
eighty year old, *agarbattis*
the Haji Ali and Mahalakshmi
lay aligned
the gods are not intolerant

dusty dusk
scatterings shadow
strings of yellow streetlights
unseen stars
lurking in the cold
beneath its warmth.

Red

Father / Today I speak to you / in a language / akin to lightness / as though a row / of red butterflies / prance inside my belly / like an unborn child / You too / were born / crying & puking / the gutters of heaven / on earth / descending like a feather / from mauve sleets / of dawn / Your mother bled / like all mothers bleed / once the umbilical cord / is cut / You once said / your birth brought a flood / with needle shaped raindrops / A birth is never liminal / but occupies all quarters / The smallest part of your brain / is where something holy / resides: / a combination of all childhood memory / fields of / rice / sugarcane / wheat / barley / cows & buffaloes tilling soil / the red light / of dawn / and tomato plants / lined like sisters braided together / When I say father / I see a young boy / scatter red seeds / into the brown soil / I see a bouquet / of tomatoes / strung like guitar chords / A crescendo / pushing over the surface / for birth / & utterance / for red / to scatter over fields / like diphthongs / preserved with symphony notes / for earth.

Cantaloupe Sundown, Kerala

the oars make a different sound
paddled over backwaters
an elephant-tail hair embossed
in a ring with bronze luminosity
braided.
the shadow of a mosquito
over blue walls of cryptic dishevel
or the reflection of a butterfly
upon a stoic monsoon puddle
harlequin shawl rests upon wood
remnant woolen strung out like grass
or chords from a harpsichord.

mimetic into shadows of dusk
rain drops from a thatched roof
refugee moths within a balmy shade
of the fringes of a house.

when the sun was out it was flaxen
but dusk has another texture
reignites bare memory of amalgams
salmon-pink emulsified musk-orange

affirms a cloudy cast beneath boats,
fishnets and fallen pale-green coconuts
where a river flows with silver lined
fishes lined as starlings on its brink.

We Shall Not Die of Exploration
But May Birth A Life

As a child, I always asked my mother
why her maternal aunt always made
a god out of situations & cursed god
afterward, when things did not go her
way. She smiled—understandingly.
I do not remember the month or
year, only charcoal black streaked skies
as butterflies retreated into their abodes
in the chiaroscuro evening & that the rain
fell slant like a descent of lightheaded jelly
beads. My mother pointed towards the
deadwoods & sang a song. I thought, this
place is an Ouija board, where lightning
would strike. When the rains were over,
two saplings arose out of a tree bark.
She left some grains of wheat in a ceramic
bowl when the sun came out again.
By noon, a blackbird had made a home
out of the ruin & my mother and I were
on the burlap path again, the closest my life
has resembled a prayer. When the voices
died, there was silence, as though there

was no chronology to god but plenitudes:
foliage, rainwater, mud, sunlight, the wind,
a sweetness on the face of my mother.

Eve, Violet Ivy

daffodil, water lily.
Once, you thought her beautiful

& the world sprung—
a dream. The first steps of a baby.

Daffodils scraped out of the earth
after a long-winter & pushed a seed

above the surface level.

—Eve, a body magnified
by the looking glass

a golden slipper. a moonless night
surrounded by cypresses.

Genesis: her soul died many times,
a strained guitar chord.

A lacquerwork box for her ashes
& she rebirthed—

daughter, mother, wife
& wife, mother, daughter again

& here: spring air & mildew,
she ran barefoot over strawberry fields

& the brown earth became pink
the color of bottled silence & bare knees

& the apple, *always the apple.*

Of Love

I know my grandmother's closet
parked with old notes, coins
and black and white photographs
with the sepia dust
of years.
How she stood amid the phylum
of fable-illustration books, guarding me.

The billowy noon
cascading into dried grass patches
over fringes of static traffic
grandmother slowly looking at
the cover prescribed to ancient
history. Our auto rickshaw
surpassing into sudden motion.

There are different ways
to feel the texture of fog
through blurred lines of memory
over a windswept barren
the trudge of silent molasses
forming within hazy lines
of water-bodies as dusk falls
upon a tired eyebrow.

Acknowledgments

Much gratitude to editors of these publications for giving prior versions of these poems a home in their respective publication.

Tethered by Borders: Rise Up Review, USA. Reprinted in Writers Resist.

Lineage: Aainanagar, India.

Bambai: VIATOR project, UK.

At night a bird perched on my window: BOMBUS Press, USA.

A Reminiscence: In Homage of: Thumb Print Magazine, India.

old Goa: The Curious Element Review, Australia.

Passion: Kitaab, Singapore.

Yarns of Shapes: Geometry, New Zealand.

Zelda: Califragile, USA.

The Unburied: Tell Me Your Story, India.

How my father prays: Figroot Press, USA. Reprinted in Best Indian Poetry 2018.

Notes de jonction: Former Cactus, UK.